Viola

T0086850

More String Time Joggers

17 pieces for flexible ensemble

Kathy and David Blackwell

Contents

Space Suite
1. March of the astronauts 2
2. Lost in space 4
3. Return to Earth 6

Travel Suite
4. Riding my bike! 10
5. Sailing home 12
6. We're all going on an aeroplane! 14

Globe-trotting Suite
7. Japanese celebration (Mura matsuri) 16
8. African song (Mweya m'tsvene) 16
9. American adventure 18

Theme Park Suite
10. Ghost train 20
11. Big Wheel waltz 22
12. Rock 'n' rollercoaster 24

Extras
13. Ev'ry time 26
14. Slovenian folk song (Kadar boš na rajžo šel) 27

Rounds
15. Carnival time 28
16. Lotus flower 28
17. Chase! 28

Illustrations by Martin Remphry

Full performances and backing tracks for all pieces are available to download from the *More String Time Joggers* Companion Website: www.oup.com/morestj

MUSIC DEPARTMENT

OXFORD
UNIVERSITY PRESS

Space Suite

1. March of the astronauts

KB & DB

This collection © Oxford University Press 2017

Printed in Great Britain
OXFORD UNIVERSITY PRESS, MUSIC DEPARTMENT, GREAT CLARENDON STREET, OXFORD OX2 6DP

The Moral Rights of the Authors have been asserted. Photocopying or arranging this copyright material is ILLEGAL.

33
3
3
f
B
40
f
f
45
51
56
mp (say)
cresc.
ff
5
4
3
2
1
Blast off!
mp (say)
cresc.
ff
5
4
3
2
1
Blast off!

2. Lost in space

KB & DB

© Oxford University Press 2017. Photocopying or arranging this copyright material is ILLEGAL.

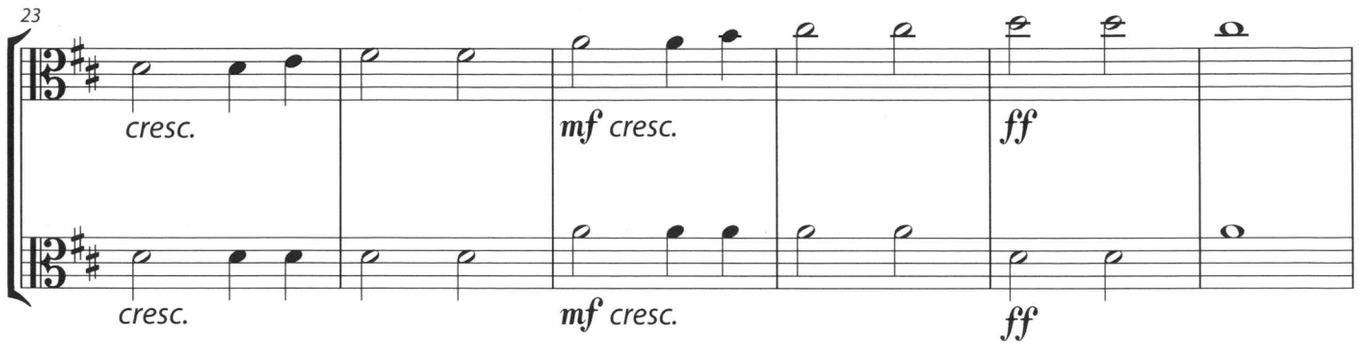
23
cresc.
mf cresc.
ff
cresc.
mf cresc.
ff

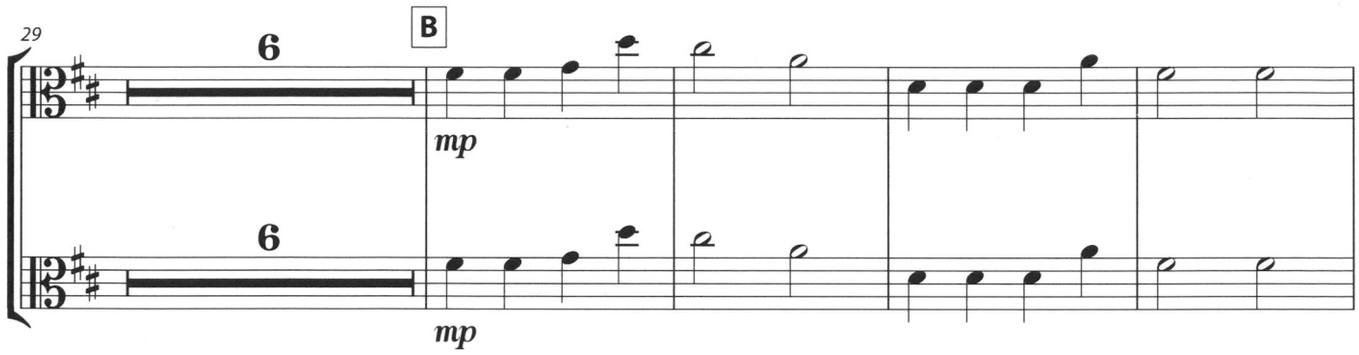
29
6
B
mp
6
mp

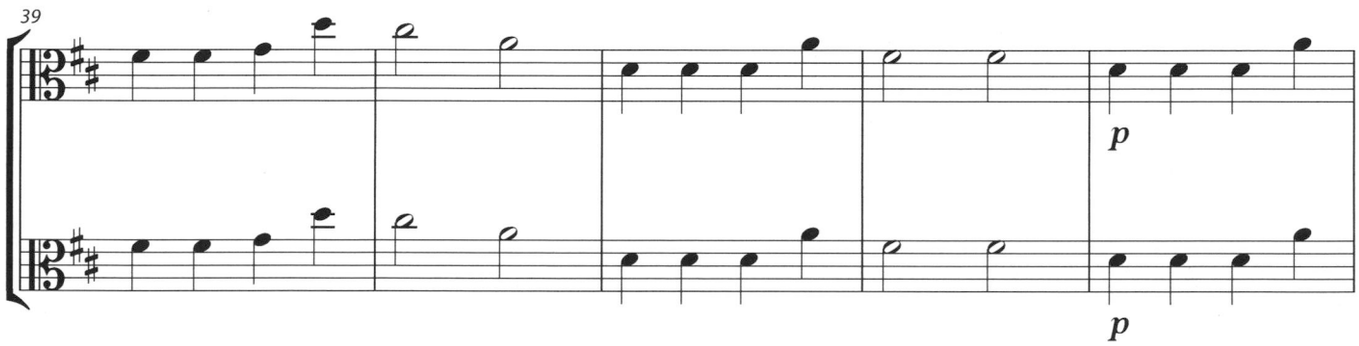
39
p
p

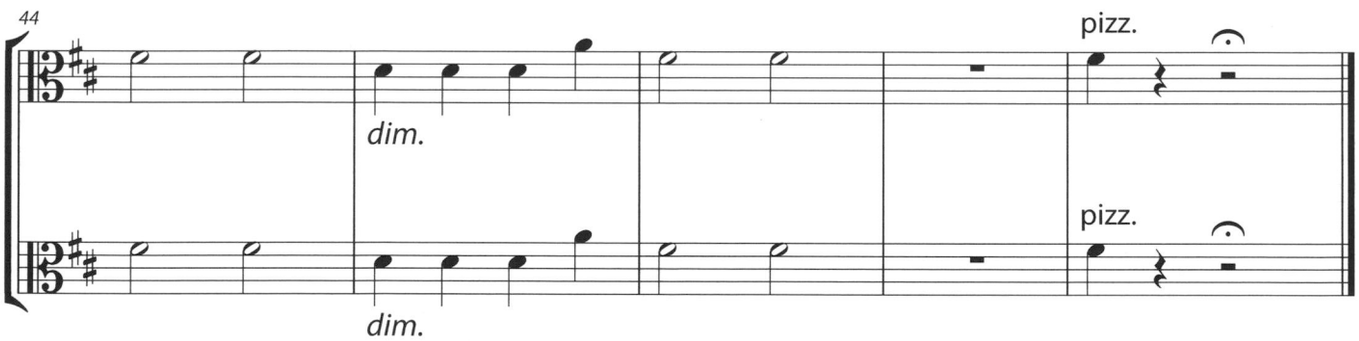
44
dim.
pizz.
dim.
pizz.

3. Return to Earth

Words and music by
KB & DB

© Oxford University Press 2017. Photocopying or arranging this copyright material is ILLEGAL.

16
ga - la - xy, so
Now we feel the pull from Earth and
gra - vi - ty, let's
fly home,
20
oh yeah!
As - te - roids and sa - tel - lites, we've
seen them all, and
23
Did you know the sun is like a
big red ball? so
Now we feel the pull from Earth and
26
gra - vi - ty, let's
fly home,
oh yeah!
4
4

B
f
33
Thou-sands of miles we've roamed, now we are head-in' home, Good-bye to ga-la-xies
f
36
light-years a-way. In-to the ro-cket ship, time now to end our trip,
C
mp
39
Hel-lo to pla-net Earth, we're on our way. Ve-nus and Mer-cu-ry,
mp
cresc.
mf
42
Nep-tune and Ju-pi-ter, Sa-turn and Ur-an-us, Plu-to and Mars,
cresc.
mf
f
45
Pla-nets both big and small, you bet we've seen them all, In all the un-i-verse
f

D

48

mp *cresc.*

we're su - per - stars! We've been in ou - ter space, meet - in' an a - lien race,

mp *cresc.*

51

mf *f* *ff*

But now we're com - in' back home to stay. Yes we are!

mf *f* *ff*

Travel Suite

4. Riding my bike!

Words and music by
KB & DB

PART 1

Lively pedal-power ♩ = 112

4 *mf*

Cycl-ing in the town I go I'm some-times fast and some-times slow I

7 *cresc.*

love to pe-dal to and fro, I'm Rid-ing my bike! Cycl-ing in the coun-try-side It

10 *f*

real-ly is a love-ly ride To pe-dal free-ly far and wide, I'm Rid-ing my bike!

13 A *mf*

Cycl-ing in the ve-lo-drome My bike is red with shi-ny chrome I'll

15 *cresc.*

soon be cycl-ing off to home, I'm Rid-ing my bike! Wind and rain or sun and shower I'll

18 *f*

keep on cycl-ing hour by hour Be-cause I've got my pe-dal-power, I'm Rid-ing my bike!

21 B *ff*

Care-ful of the lor-ries and don't get in their way, Then no-bo-dy wor-ries as you

24

cy-cle each day. Care-ful of the bus-es as they crawl up the street,

27 C *mf*

Then no-bo-dy fus-ses as you pe-dal so neat! Cycl-ing's fun and ve-ry green It

© Oxford University Press 2017. Photocopying or arranging this copyright material is ILLEGAL.

PART 2

Lively pedal-power ♩ = 112

5. Sailing home

KB & DB

© Oxford University Press 2017. Photocopying or arranging this copyright material is ILLEGAL.

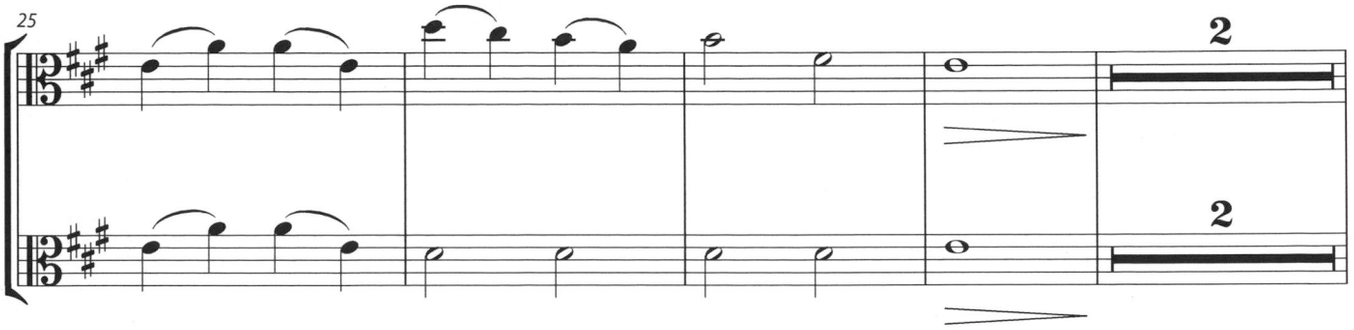
25
2
2

B
31
mp
mp

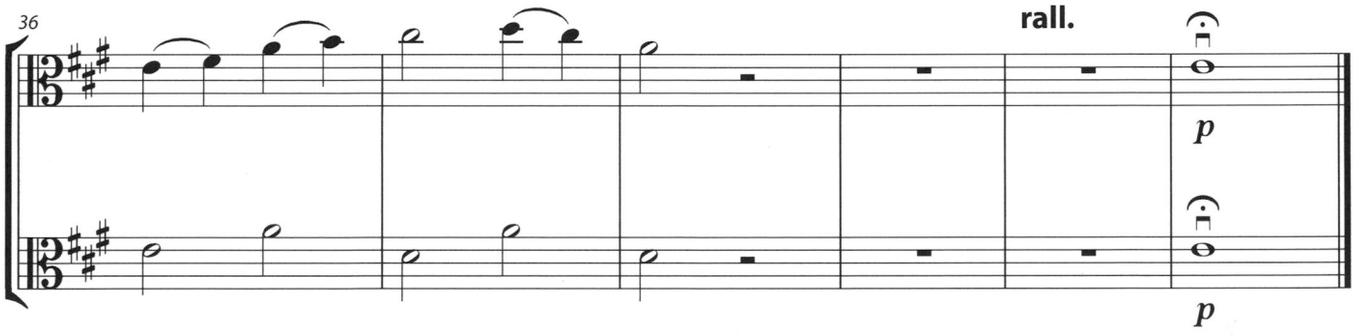
36
rall.
p
p

CAPTAIN CROTCHET

6. We're all going on an aeroplane!

KB & DB

© Oxford University Press 2017. Photocopying or arranging this copyright material is ILLEGAL.

21
B
f
f
26
31
cresc.
cresc.
36
1.
to bar 41
2.
Fine
ff
ff
41
C
1/2
p
mp
cresc.
46
mf
p
mp
52
D.𝄋. al Fine
cresc.
mf

Globe-trotting Suite

7. Japanese celebration (Mura matsuri)

Japanese trad.
arr. KB & DB

8. African song (Mweya m'tsvene)

Shona trad., Zimbabwe
arr. KB & DB

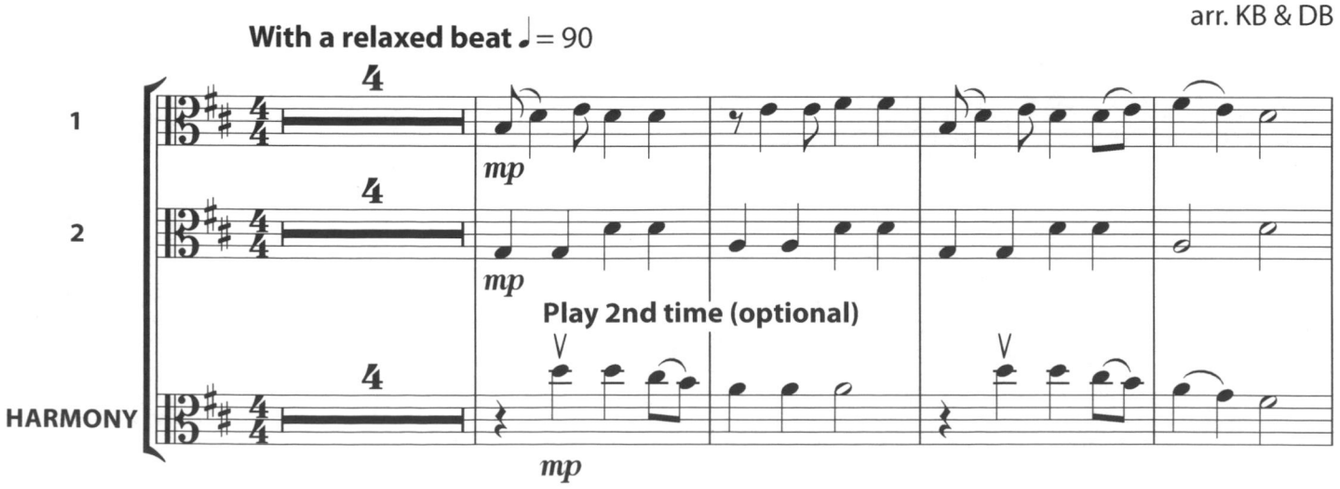

All pieces © Oxford University Press 2017. Photocopying or arranging this copyright material is ILLEGAL.

9
13
A
1
mf
2
mf
17
21
B
All
Gently tap wood of instrument
25
Hear the djem-be, play-ing soft-ly, hear the djem-be in Af-ri-ca.
29
rall.
Hear the djem-be, play-ing soft-ly, hear the djem-be in Af-ri-ca.

9. American adventure

© Oxford University Press 2017. Photocopying or arranging this copyright material is ILLEGAL.

30
f
f
36
41
ff
ff
45
C Sourwood Mountain
1
f
2
f
Li'l Liza Jane (Optional harmony)
HAR.
f
49
53
All
ff
1
2

Theme Park Suite

10. Ghost train

KB & DB

© Oxford University Press 2017. Photocopying or arranging this copyright material is ILLEGAL.

25
B
f
p
f
f
f
p
f
f
30
p
p
35
C
cresc.
f
f
cresc.
f
f
41
D
rall.
Spookily ♩ = 88
p
mf
cresc.
f
p
mf
cresc.
f
47
pizz.
ff
p
Boo!
pizz.
ff
p
Boo!

11. Big Wheel waltz

KB & DB

Gently circling ♩ = 100

1

2

4

mp

mf

10

17

A

Big Wheel! *

Big Wheel! *

24

32

B

* In the rests in section A make a circle in the air with the bow, like a Big Wheel!

© Oxford University Press 2017. Photocopying or arranging this copyright material is ILLEGAL.

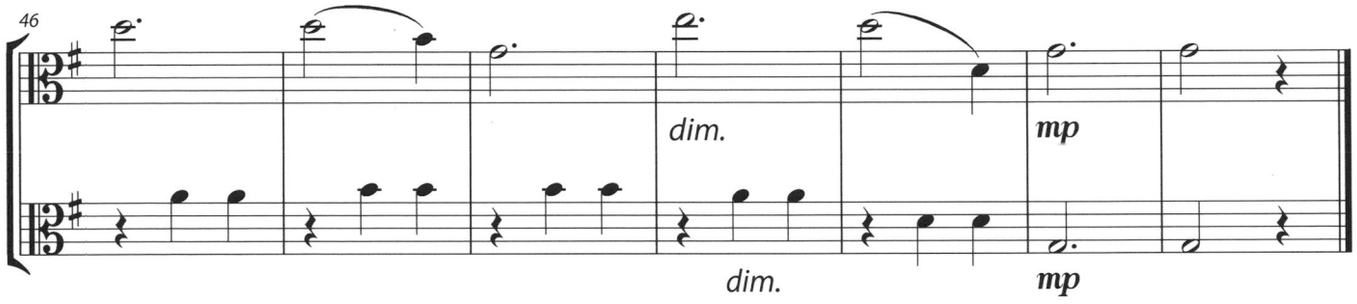

OPTIONAL HARMONY PART

Gently circling ♩ = 100

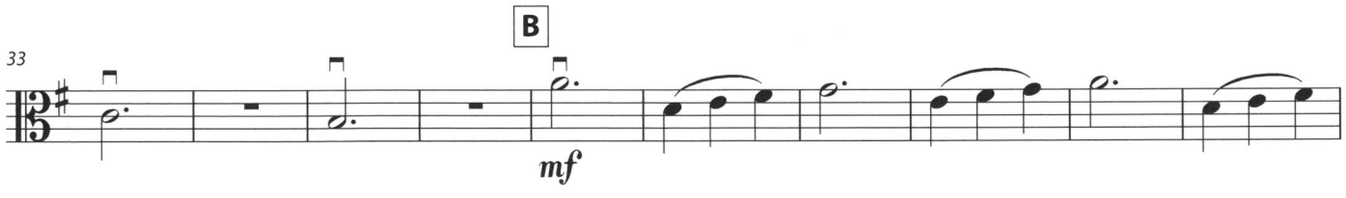

* In the rests in section A make a circle in the air with the bow, like a Big Wheel!

12. Rock 'n' rollercoaster

Words and music by
KB & DB

© Oxford University Press 2017. Photocopying or arranging this copyright material is ILLEGAL.

22
touch the sky, we're spin-nin' so far from the ground. Step a-board the rol-ler-coast-er
27
B
f
ride!
Twist and turn, time to rock and roll,
f
rol-ler-coast-er ride!
33
Dip and dive, time to rock and roll,
Step a-board the
Rol-ler-coast-er ride!
38
mp
C
rol-ler-coast-er ride!
Step a-board the rol-ler-coast-er ride!
mp
44
f
ff
Step a-board the rol-ler-coast-er ride, it's rock-in'!
f
ff

Extras

13. Ev'ry time

Jamaican trad.
arr. and with words by KB & DB

MELODY

© Oxford University Press 2017. Photocopying or arranging this copyright material is ILLEGAL.

14. Slovenian folk song (Kadar boš na rajžo šel)

Slovenian trad.
arr. KB & DB

© Oxford University Press 2017. Photocopying or arranging this copyright material is ILLEGAL.

Rounds

15. Carnival time

16. Lotus flower

17. Chase!

All pieces © Oxford University Press 2017. Photocopying or arranging this copyright material is ILLEGAL.